BIC
INFOR

GW01445177

YEAR:	
MAKE:	
MODEL:	
FRAME #:	
OWNER:	
OWNER E-MAIL:	
PURCHASE DATE:	
PURCHASE CONDITION:	
PURCHASED FROM:	

BICYCLE SAFETY CHECK

SAFETY ITEM	✓	✓	✓
Axles Oiled & Adjusted			
Bell or Horn in Good Working Condition			
Bottom Bracket Bearing Turns Freely			
Brakes Adjusted			
Cables Taut, Unbroken & Unfrayed			
Chain Lubricated & Tension Adjusted			
Chain Protector Solid & Adjusted			
Chainrings & Bolts Tight & Good Condition			
Crank Arms Tight & Good Condition			
Derailleur & Shift Levers Checked			
Fenders Tightly Attached & Not Rubbing Tires			
Fork Tight & Turns Freely			
Frame in Good Structural Condition			
Front Fork in Good Structural Condition			
Handlebars & Grips Tight			

BICYCLE SAFETY CHECK

SAFETY ITEM	✓	✓	✓
Handlebars Adjusted			
Headset Bearing Lubricated & Freely Turns			
Lights in Good Condition			
Pedals Tightly Attached & Lubricated			
Quick Release Tension Checked			
Reflectors in Good Condition			
Rims in Good Structural Condition			
Saddle Tight & Adjusted			
Spokes Tight, Upbroken & Unbent			
Sprocket Adjusted			
Tires Properly Inflated with Tread & No Cuts			
Wheel Bearings Lubricated & Adjusted			
Wheel Nuts Tight			
Wheels Aligned, No Broken or Loose Spokes			
Wheels Centered & Straight			

BICYCLE SAFETY CHECK

SAFETY ITEM	✓	✓	✓
Axles Oiled & Adjusted			
Bell or Horn in Good Working Condition			
Bottom Bracket Bearing Turns Freely			
Brakes Adjusted			
Cables Taut, Unbroken & Unfrayed			
Chain Lubricated & Tension Adjusted			
Chain Protector Solid & Adjusted			
Chainrings & Bolts Tight & Good Condition			
Crank Arms Tight & Good Condition			
Derailleur & Shift Levers Checked			
Fenders Tightly Attached & Not Rubbing Tires			
Fork Tight & Turns Freely			
Frame in Good Structural Condition			
Front Fork in Good Structural Condition			
Handlebars & Grips Tight			

BICYCLE SAFETY CHECK

SAFETY ITEM	✓	✓	✓
Handlebars Adjusted			
Headset Bearing Lubricated & Freely Turns			
Lights in Good Condition			
Pedals Tightly Attached & Lubricated			
Quick Release Tension Checked			
Reflectors in Good Condition			
Rims in Good Structural Condition			
Saddle Tight & Adjusted			
Spokes Tight, Upbroken & Unbent			
Sprocket Adjusted			
Tires Properly Inflated with Tread & No Cuts			
Wheel Bearings Lubricated & Adjusted			
Wheel Nuts Tight			
Wheels Aligned, No Broken or Loose Spokes			
Wheels Centered & Straight			

BICYCLE SAFETY CHECK

SAFETY ITEM	✓	✓	✓
Axles Oiled & Adjusted			
Bell or Horn in Good Working Condition			
Bottom Bracket Bearing Turns Freely			
Brakes Adjusted			
Cables Taut, Unbroken & Unfrayed			
Chain Lubricated & Tension Adjusted			
Chain Protector Solid & Adjusted			
Chainrings & Bolts Tight & Good Condition			
Crank Arms Tight & Good Condition			
Derailleur & Shift Levers Checked			
Fenders Tightly Attached & Not Rubbing Tires			
Fork Tight & Turns Freely			
Frame in Good Structural Condition			
Front Fork in Good Structural Condition			
Handlebars & Grips Tight			

BICYCLE SAFETY CHECK

SAFETY ITEM	✓	✓	✓
Handlebars Adjusted			
Headset Bearing Lubricated & Freely Turns			
Lights in Good Condition			
Pedals Tightly Attached & Lubricated			
Quick Release Tension Checked			
Reflectors in Good Condition			
Rims in Good Structural Condition			
Saddle Tight & Adjusted			
Spokes Tight, Upbroken & Unbent			
Sprocket Adjusted			
Tires Properly Inflated with Tread & No Cuts			
Wheel Bearings Lubricated & Adjusted			
Wheel Nuts Tight			
Wheels Aligned, No Broken or Loose Spokes			
Wheels Centered & Straight			

BICYCLE SAFETY CHECK

SAFETY ITEM	✓	✓	✓
Axles Oiled & Adjusted			
Bell or Horn in Good Working Condition			
Bottom Bracket Bearing Turns Freely			
Brakes Adjusted			
Cables Taut, Unbroken & Unfrayed			
Chain Lubricated & Tension Adjusted			
Chain Protector Solid & Adjusted			
Chainrings & Bolts Tight & Good Condition			
Crank Arms Tight & Good Condition			
Derailleur & Shift Levers Checked			
Fenders Tightly Attached & Not Rubbing Tires			
Fork Tight & Turns Freely			
Frame in Good Structural Condition			
Front Fork in Good Structural Condition			
Handlebars & Grips Tight			

BICYCLE SAFETY CHECK

SAFETY ITEM	✓	✓	✓
Handlebars Adjusted			
Headset Bearing Lubricated & Freely Turns			
Lights in Good Condition			
Pedals Tightly Attached & Lubricated			
Quick Release Tension Checked			
Reflectors in Good Condition			
Rims in Good Structural Condition			
Saddle Tight & Adjusted			
Spokes Tight, Upbroken & Unbent			
Sprocket Adjusted			
Tires Properly Inflated with Tread & No Cuts			
Wheel Bearings Lubricated & Adjusted			
Wheel Nuts Tight			
Wheels Aligned, No Broken or Loose Spokes			
Wheels Centered & Straight			

BICYCLE SAFETY CHECK

SAFETY ITEM	✓	✓	✓
Axles Oiled & Adjusted			
Bell or Horn in Good Working Condition			
Bottom Bracket Bearing Turns Freely			
Brakes Adjusted			
Cables Taut, Unbroken & Unfrayed			
Chain Lubricated & Tension Adjusted			
Chain Protector Solid & Adjusted			
Chainrings & Bolts Tight & Good Condition			
Crank Arms Tight & Good Condition			
Derailleur & Shift Levers Checked			
Fenders Tightly Attached & Not Rubbing Tires			
Fork Tight & Turns Freely			
Frame in Good Structural Condition			
Front Fork in Good Structural Condition			
Handlebars & Grips Tight			

BICYCLE SAFETY CHECK

SAFETY ITEM	✓	✓	✓
Handlebars Adjusted			
Headset Bearing Lubricated & Freely Turns			
Lights in Good Condition			
Pedals Tightly Attached & Lubricated			
Quick Release Tension Checked			
Reflectors in Good Condition			
Rims in Good Structural Condition			
Saddle Tight & Adjusted			
Spokes Tight, Upbroken & Unbent			
Sprocket Adjusted			
Tires Properly Inflated with Tread & No Cuts			
Wheel Bearings Lubricated & Adjusted			
Wheel Nuts Tight			
Wheels Aligned, No Broken or Loose Spokes			
Wheels Centered & Straight			

BICYCLE SAFETY CHECK

SAFETY ITEM	✓	✓	✓
Axles Oiled & Adjusted			
Bell or Horn in Good Working Condition			
Bottom Bracket Bearing Turns Freely			
Brakes Adjusted			
Cables Taut, Unbroken & Unfrayed			
Chain Lubricated & Tension Adjusted			
Chain Protector Solid & Adjusted			
Chainrings & Bolts Tight & Good Condition			
Crank Arms Tight & Good Condition			
Derailleur & Shift Levers Checked			
Fenders Tightly Attached & Not Rubbing Tires			
Fork Tight & Turns Freely			
Frame in Good Structural Condition			
Front Fork in Good Structural Condition			
Handlebars & Grips Tight			

BICYCLE SAFETY CHECK

SAFETY ITEM	✓	✓	✓
Handlebars Adjusted			
Headset Bearing Lubricated & Freely Turns			
Lights in Good Condition			
Pedals Tightly Attached & Lubricated			
Quick Release Tension Checked			
Reflectors in Good Condition			
Rims in Good Structural Condition			
Saddle Tight & Adjusted			
Spokes Tight, Upbroken & Unbent			
Sprocket Adjusted			
Tires Properly Inflated with Tread & No Cuts			
Wheel Bearings Lubricated & Adjusted			
Wheel Nuts Tight			
Wheels Aligned, No Broken or Loose Spokes			
Wheels Centered & Straight			

BICYCLE SAFETY CHECK

SAFETY ITEM	✓	✓	✓
Axles Oiled & Adjusted			
Bell or Horn in Good Working Condition			
Bottom Bracket Bearing Turns Freely			
Brakes Adjusted			
Cables Taut, Unbroken & Unfrayed			
Chain Lubricated & Tension Adjusted			
Chain Protector Solid & Adjusted			
Chainrings & Bolts Tight & Good Condition			
Crank Arms Tight & Good Condition			
Derailleur & Shift Levers Checked			
Fenders Tightly Attached & Not Rubbing Tires			
Fork Tight & Turns Freely			
Frame in Good Structural Condition			
Front Fork in Good Structural Condition			
Handlebars & Grips Tight			

BICYCLE SAFETY CHECK

SAFETY ITEM	✓	✓	✓
Handlebars Adjusted			
Headset Bearing Lubricated & Freely Turns			
Lights in Good Condition			
Pedals Tightly Attached & Lubricated			
Quick Release Tension Checked			
Reflectors in Good Condition			
Rims in Good Structural Condition			
Saddle Tight & Adjusted			
Spokes Tight, Upbroken & Unbent			
Sprocket Adjusted			
Tires Properly Inflated with Tread & No Cuts			
Wheel Bearings Lubricated & Adjusted			
Wheel Nuts Tight			
Wheels Aligned, No Broken or Loose Spokes			
Wheels Centered & Straight			

BICYCLE SAFETY CHECK

SAFETY ITEM	✓	✓	✓
Axles Oiled & Adjusted			
Bell or Horn in Good Working Condition			
Bottom Bracket Bearing Turns Freely			
Brakes Adjusted			
Cables Taut, Unbroken & Unfrayed			
Chain Lubricated & Tension Adjusted			
Chain Protector Solid & Adjusted			
Chainrings & Bolts Tight & Good Condition			
Crank Arms Tight & Good Condition			
Derailleur & Shift Levers Checked			
Fenders Tightly Attached & Not Rubbing Tires			
Fork Tight & Turns Freely			
Frame in Good Structural Condition			
Front Fork in Good Structural Condition			
Handlebars & Grips Tight			

BICYCLE SAFETY CHECK

SAFETY ITEM	✓	✓	✓
Handlebars Adjusted			
Headset Bearing Lubricated & Freely Turns			
Lights in Good Condition			
Pedals Tightly Attached & Lubricated			
Quick Release Tension Checked			
Reflectors in Good Condition			
Rims in Good Structural Condition			
Saddle Tight & Adjusted			
Spokes Tight, Upbroken & Unbent			
Sprocket Adjusted			
Tires Properly Inflated with Tread & No Cuts			
Wheel Bearings Lubricated & Adjusted			
Wheel Nuts Tight			
Wheels Aligned, No Broken or Loose Spokes			
Wheels Centered & Straight			

BICYCLE SAFETY CHECK

SAFETY ITEM	✓	✓	✓
Axles Oiled & Adjusted			
Bell or Horn in Good Working Condition			
Bottom Bracket Bearing Turns Freely			
Brakes Adjusted			
Cables Taut, Unbroken & Unfrayed			
Chain Lubricated & Tension Adjusted			
Chain Protector Solid & Adjusted			
Chainrings & Bolts Tight & Good Condition			
Crank Arms Tight & Good Condition			
Derailleur & Shift Levers Checked			
Fenders Tightly Attached & Not Rubbing Tires			
Fork Tight & Turns Freely			
Frame in Good Structural Condition			
Front Fork in Good Structural Condition			
Handlebars & Grips Tight			

BICYCLE SAFETY CHECK

SAFETY ITEM	✓	✓	✓
Handlebars Adjusted			
Headset Bearing Lubricated & Freely Turns			
Lights in Good Condition			
Pedals Tightly Attached & Lubricated			
Quick Release Tension Checked			
Reflectors in Good Condition			
Rims in Good Structural Condition			
Saddle Tight & Adjusted			
Spokes Tight, Upbroken & Unbent			
Sprocket Adjusted			
Tires Properly Inflated with Tread & No Cuts			
Wheel Bearings Lubricated & Adjusted			
Wheel Nuts Tight			
Wheels Aligned, No Broken or Loose Spokes			
Wheels Centered & Straight			

BICYCLE SAFETY CHECK

SAFETY ITEM	✓	✓	✓
Axles Oiled & Adjusted			
Bell or Horn in Good Working Condition			
Bottom Bracket Bearing Turns Freely			
Brakes Adjusted			
Cables Taut, Unbroken & Unfrayed			
Chain Lubricated & Tension Adjusted			
Chain Protector Solid & Adjusted			
Chainrings & Bolts Tight & Good Condition			
Crank Arms Tight & Good Condition			
Derailleur & Shift Levers Checked			
Fenders Tightly Attached & Not Rubbing Tires			
Fork Tight & Turns Freely			
Frame in Good Structural Condition			
Front Fork in Good Structural Condition			
Handlebars & Grips Tight			

BICYCLE SAFETY CHECK

SAFETY ITEM	✓	✓	✓
Handlebars Adjusted			
Headset Bearing Lubricated & Freely Turns			
Lights in Good Condition			
Pedals Tightly Attached & Lubricated			
Quick Release Tension Checked			
Reflectors in Good Condition			
Rims in Good Structural Condition			
Saddle Tight & Adjusted			
Spokes Tight, Upbroken & Unbent			
Sprocket Adjusted			
Tires Properly Inflated with Tread & No Cuts			
Wheel Bearings Lubricated & Adjusted			
Wheel Nuts Tight			
Wheels Aligned, No Broken or Loose Spokes			
Wheels Centered & Straight			

BICYCLE SAFETY CHECK

SAFETY ITEM	✓	✓	✓
Axles Oiled & Adjusted			
Bell or Horn in Good Working Condition			
Bottom Bracket Bearing Turns Freely			
Brakes Adjusted			
Cables Taut, Unbroken & Unfrayed			
Chain Lubricated & Tension Adjusted			
Chain Protector Solid & Adjusted			
Chainrings & Bolts Tight & Good Condition			
Crank Arms Tight & Good Condition			
Derailleur & Shift Levers Checked			
Fenders Tightly Attached & Not Rubbing Tires			
Fork Tight & Turns Freely			
Frame in Good Structural Condition			
Front Fork in Good Structural Condition			
Handlebars & Grips Tight			

BICYCLE SAFETY CHECK

SAFETY ITEM	✓	✓	✓
Handlebars Adjusted			
Headset Bearing Lubricated & Freely Turns			
Lights in Good Condition			
Pedals Tightly Attached & Lubricated			
Quick Release Tension Checked			
Reflectors in Good Condition			
Rims in Good Structural Condition			
Saddle Tight & Adjusted			
Spokes Tight, Upbroken & Unbent			
Sprocket Adjusted			
Tires Properly Inflated with Tread & No Cuts			
Wheel Bearings Lubricated & Adjusted			
Wheel Nuts Tight			
Wheels Aligned, No Broken or Loose Spokes			
Wheels Centered & Straight			

BICYCLE SAFETY CHECK

SAFETY ITEM	✓	✓	✓
Axles Oiled & Adjusted			
Bell or Horn in Good Working Condition			
Bottom Bracket Bearing Turns Freely			
Brakes Adjusted			
Cables Taut, Unbroken & Unfrayed			
Chain Lubricated & Tension Adjusted			
Chain Protector Solid & Adjusted			
Chainrings & Bolts Tight & Good Condition			
Crank Arms Tight & Good Condition			
Derailleur & Shift Levers Checked			
Fenders Tightly Attached & Not Rubbing Tires			
Fork Tight & Turns Freely			
Frame in Good Structural Condition			
Front Fork in Good Structural Condition			
Handlebars & Grips Tight			

BICYCLE SAFETY CHECK

SAFETY ITEM	✓	✓	✓
Handlebars Adjusted			
Headset Bearing Lubricated & Freely Turns			
Lights in Good Condition			
Pedals Tightly Attached & Lubricated			
Quick Release Tension Checked			
Reflectors in Good Condition			
Rims in Good Structural Condition			
Saddle Tight & Adjusted			
Spokes Tight, Upbroken & Unbent			
Sprocket Adjusted			
Tires Properly Inflated with Tread & No Cuts			
Wheel Bearings Lubricated & Adjusted			
Wheel Nuts Tight			
Wheels Aligned, No Broken or Loose Spokes			
Wheels Centered & Straight			

BICYCLE SAFETY CHECK

SAFETY ITEM	✓	✓	✓
Axles Oiled & Adjusted			
Bell or Horn in Good Working Condition			
Bottom Bracket Bearing Turns Freely			
Brakes Adjusted			
Cables Taut, Unbroken & Unfrayed			
Chain Lubricated & Tension Adjusted			
Chain Protector Solid & Adjusted			
Chainrings & Bolts Tight & Good Condition			
Crank Arms Tight & Good Condition			
Derailleur & Shift Levers Checked			
Fenders Tightly Attached & Not Rubbing Tires			
Fork Tight & Turns Freely			
Frame in Good Structural Condition			
Front Fork in Good Structural Condition			
Handlebars & Grips Tight			

BICYCLE SAFETY CHECK

SAFETY ITEM	✓	✓	✓
Handlebars Adjusted			
Headset Bearing Lubricated & Freely Turns			
Lights in Good Condition			
Pedals Tightly Attached & Lubricated			
Quick Release Tension Checked			
Reflectors in Good Condition			
Rims in Good Structural Condition			
Saddle Tight & Adjusted			
Spokes Tight, Upbroken & Unbent			
Sprocket Adjusted			
Tires Properly Inflated with Tread & No Cuts			
Wheel Bearings Lubricated & Adjusted			
Wheel Nuts Tight			
Wheels Aligned, No Broken or Loose Spokes			
Wheels Centered & Straight			

BICYCLE SAFETY CHECK

SAFETY ITEM	✓	✓	✓
Axles Oiled & Adjusted			
Bell or Horn in Good Working Condition			
Bottom Bracket Bearing Turns Freely			
Brakes Adjusted			
Cables Taut, Unbroken & Unfrayed			
Chain Lubricated & Tension Adjusted			
Chain Protector Solid & Adjusted			
Chainrings & Bolts Tight & Good Condition			
Crank Arms Tight & Good Condition			
Derailleur & Shift Levers Checked			
Fenders Tightly Attached & Not Rubbing Tires			
Fork Tight & Turns Freely			
Frame in Good Structural Condition			
Front Fork in Good Structural Condition			
Handlebars & Grips Tight			

BICYCLE SAFETY CHECK

SAFETY ITEM	✓	✓	✓
Handlebars Adjusted			
Headset Bearing Lubricated & Freely Turns			
Lights in Good Condition			
Pedals Tightly Attached & Lubricated			
Quick Release Tension Checked			
Reflectors in Good Condition			
Rims in Good Structural Condition			
Saddle Tight & Adjusted			
Spokes Tight, Upbroken & Unbent			
Sprocket Adjusted			
Tires Properly Inflated with Tread & No Cuts			
Wheel Bearings Lubricated & Adjusted			
Wheel Nuts Tight			
Wheels Aligned, No Broken or Loose Spokes			
Wheels Centered & Straight			

BICYCLE SAFETY CHECK

SAFETY ITEM	✓	✓	✓
Axles Oiled & Adjusted			
Bell or Horn in Good Working Condition			
Bottom Bracket Bearing Turns Freely			
Brakes Adjusted			
Cables Taut, Unbroken & Unfrayed			
Chain Lubricated & Tension Adjusted			
Chain Protector Solid & Adjusted			
Chainrings & Bolts Tight & Good Condition			
Crank Arms Tight & Good Condition			
Derailleur & Shift Levers Checked			
Fenders Tightly Attached & Not Rubbing Tires			
Fork Tight & Turns Freely			
Frame in Good Structural Condition			
Front Fork in Good Structural Condition			
Handlebars & Grips Tight			

BICYCLE SAFETY CHECK

SAFETY ITEM	✓	✓	✓
Handlebars Adjusted			
Headset Bearing Lubricated & Freely Turns			
Lights in Good Condition			
Pedals Tightly Attached & Lubricated			
Quick Release Tension Checked			
Reflectors in Good Condition			
Rims in Good Structural Condition			
Saddle Tight & Adjusted			
Spokes Tight, Upbroken & Unbent			
Sprocket Adjusted			
Tires Properly Inflated with Tread & No Cuts			
Wheel Bearings Lubricated & Adjusted			
Wheel Nuts Tight			
Wheels Aligned, No Broken or Loose Spokes			
Wheels Centered & Straight			

BICYCLE SAFETY CHECK

SAFETY ITEM	✓	✓	✓
Axles Oiled & Adjusted			
Bell or Horn in Good Working Condition			
Bottom Bracket Bearing Turns Freely			
Brakes Adjusted			
Cables Taut, Unbroken & Unfrayed			
Chain Lubricated & Tension Adjusted			
Chain Protector Solid & Adjusted			
Chainrings & Bolts Tight & Good Condition			
Crank Arms Tight & Good Condition			
Derailleur & Shift Levers Checked			
Fenders Tightly Attached & Not Rubbing Tires			
Fork Tight & Turns Freely			
Frame in Good Structural Condition			
Front Fork in Good Structural Condition			
Handlebars & Grips Tight			

BICYCLE SAFETY CHECK

SAFETY ITEM	✓	✓	✓
Handlebars Adjusted			
Headset Bearing Lubricated & Freely Turns			
Lights in Good Condition			
Pedals Tightly Attached & Lubricated			
Quick Release Tension Checked			
Reflectors in Good Condition			
Rims in Good Structural Condition			
Saddle Tight & Adjusted			
Spokes Tight, Upbroken & Unbent			
Sprocket Adjusted			
Tires Properly Inflated with Tread & No Cuts			
Wheel Bearings Lubricated & Adjusted			
Wheel Nuts Tight			
Wheels Aligned, No Broken or Loose Spokes			
Wheels Centered & Straight			

BICYCLE SAFETY CHECK

SAFETY ITEM	✓	✓	✓
Axles Oiled & Adjusted			
Bell or Horn in Good Working Condition			
Bottom Bracket Bearing Turns Freely			
Brakes Adjusted			
Cables Taut, Unbroken & Unfrayed			
Chain Lubricated & Tension Adjusted			
Chain Protector Solid & Adjusted			
Chainrings & Bolts Tight & Good Condition			
Crank Arms Tight & Good Condition			
Derailleur & Shift Levers Checked			
Fenders Tightly Attached & Not Rubbing Tires			
Fork Tight & Turns Freely			
Frame in Good Structural Condition			
Front Fork in Good Structural Condition			
Handlebars & Grips Tight			

BICYCLE SAFETY CHECK

SAFETY ITEM	✓	✓	✓
Handlebars Adjusted			
Headset Bearing Lubricated & Freely Turns			
Lights in Good Condition			
Pedals Tightly Attached & Lubricated			
Quick Release Tension Checked			
Reflectors in Good Condition			
Rims in Good Structural Condition			
Saddle Tight & Adjusted			
Spokes Tight, Upbroken & Unbent			
Sprocket Adjusted			
Tires Properly Inflated with Tread & No Cuts			
Wheel Bearings Lubricated & Adjusted			
Wheel Nuts Tight			
Wheels Aligned, No Broken or Loose Spokes			
Wheels Centered & Straight			

BICYCLE SAFETY CHECK

SAFETY ITEM	✓	✓	✓
Axles Oiled & Adjusted			
Bell or Horn in Good Working Condition			
Bottom Bracket Bearing Turns Freely			
Brakes Adjusted			
Cables Taut, Unbroken & Unfrayed			
Chain Lubricated & Tension Adjusted			
Chain Protector Solid & Adjusted			
Chainrings & Bolts Tight & Good Condition			
Crank Arms Tight & Good Condition			
Derailleur & Shift Levers Checked			
Fenders Tightly Attached & Not Rubbing Tires			
Fork Tight & Turns Freely			
Frame in Good Structural Condition			
Front Fork in Good Structural Condition			
Handlebars & Grips Tight			

BICYCLE SAFETY CHECK

SAFETY ITEM	✓	✓	✓
Handlebars Adjusted			
Headset Bearing Lubricated & Freely Turns			
Lights in Good Condition			
Pedals Tightly Attached & Lubricated			
Quick Release Tension Checked			
Reflectors in Good Condition			
Rims in Good Structural Condition			
Saddle Tight & Adjusted			
Spokes Tight, Upbroken & Unbent			
Sprocket Adjusted			
Tires Properly Inflated with Tread & No Cuts			
Wheel Bearings Lubricated & Adjusted			
Wheel Nuts Tight			
Wheels Aligned, No Broken or Loose Spokes			
Wheels Centered & Straight			

BICYCLE SAFETY CHECK

SAFETY ITEM	✓	✓	✓
Axles Oiled & Adjusted			
Bell or Horn in Good Working Condition			
Bottom Bracket Bearing Turns Freely			
Brakes Adjusted			
Cables Taut, Unbroken & Unfrayed			
Chain Lubricated & Tension Adjusted			
Chain Protector Solid & Adjusted			
Chainrings & Bolts Tight & Good Condition			
Crank Arms Tight & Good Condition			
Derailleur & Shift Levers Checked			
Fenders Tightly Attached & Not Rubbing Tires			
Fork Tight & Turns Freely			
Frame in Good Structural Condition			
Front Fork in Good Structural Condition			
Handlebars & Grips Tight			

BICYCLE SAFETY CHECK

SAFETY ITEM	✓	✓	✓
Handlebars Adjusted			
Headset Bearing Lubricated & Freely Turns			
Lights in Good Condition			
Pedals Tightly Attached & Lubricated			
Quick Release Tension Checked			
Reflectors in Good Condition			
Rims in Good Structural Condition			
Saddle Tight & Adjusted			
Spokes Tight, Upbroken & Unbent			
Sprocket Adjusted			
Tires Properly Inflated with Tread & No Cuts			
Wheel Bearings Lubricated & Adjusted			
Wheel Nuts Tight			
Wheels Aligned, No Broken or Loose Spokes			
Wheels Centered & Straight			

BICYCLE SAFETY CHECK

SAFETY ITEM	✓	✓	✓
Axles Oiled & Adjusted			
Bell or Horn in Good Working Condition			
Bottom Bracket Bearing Turns Freely			
Brakes Adjusted			
Cables Taut, Unbroken & Unfrayed			
Chain Lubricated & Tension Adjusted			
Chain Protector Solid & Adjusted			
Chainrings & Bolts Tight & Good Condition			
Crank Arms Tight & Good Condition			
Derailleur & Shift Levers Checked			
Fenders Tightly Attached & Not Rubbing Tires			
Fork Tight & Turns Freely			
Frame in Good Structural Condition			
Front Fork in Good Structural Condition			
Handlebars & Grips Tight			

BICYCLE SAFETY CHECK

SAFETY ITEM	✓	✓	✓
Handlebars Adjusted			
Headset Bearing Lubricated & Freely Turns			
Lights in Good Condition			
Pedals Tightly Attached & Lubricated			
Quick Release Tension Checked			
Reflectors in Good Condition			
Rims in Good Structural Condition			
Saddle Tight & Adjusted			
Spokes Tight, Upbroken & Unbent			
Sprocket Adjusted			
Tires Properly Inflated with Tread & No Cuts			
Wheel Bearings Lubricated & Adjusted			
Wheel Nuts Tight			
Wheels Aligned, No Broken or Loose Spokes			
Wheels Centered & Straight			

MONTHLY MAINTENANCE CHECK

YEAR:	JANUARY	FEBRUARY	MARCH	APRIL	MAY	JUNE	JULY	AUGUST	SEPTEMBER	OCTOBER	NOVEMBER	DECEMBER
Brake Cables: Lube												
Brake Pads, Cable Clamp & Levers												
Chain, Cogs & Chainrings												
Chain: Check for Wear												
Derailleur: Lube Pivots & Pulleys												
Drivetrain: Degrease & Lube												
Pedals: Lube & Tighten												
Saddle												
Shift Cables: Lube												
Structural Inspection												
Suspension Bolts & Forks												
Suspension Sliders: Lube												
Tighten Nuts, Bolts &Fasteners												
Wheels & Tires: Condition, Pressure & Spokes												
Wipe Down & Clean Bike												

ANNUAL MAINTENANCE CHECK

SERVICE ITEM	✓
Accessories: Check, Update or Replacement	
Bleed Hydraulic Brakes	
Bottom Bracket Overhaul or Replacement	
Brake Pad Replacement	
Cable & Housing Replacement	
Chain: Deep clean or Replacement	
Derailleur: Clean Jockey Wheels	
Frame & Dropper Post Overhaul	
Frame: Clean & Wax	
Handlebar Tape or Grips Replacement	
Headset Overhaul	
Hubs Overhaul	
Pedal Overhaul	
Shock Oil Replacement	
Suspension Pivots: Clean & Grease	
Tire Replacement	
Tubeless Tire Sealant Replacement	
Wheels: True Alignment & Tension	

MONTHLY MAINTENANCE CHECK

YEAR:	JANUARY	FEBRUARY	MARCH	APRIL	MAY	JUNE	JULY	AUGUST	SEPTEMBER	OCTOBER	NOVEMBER	DECEMBER
Brake Cables: Lube												
Brake Pads, Cable Clamp & Levers												
Chain, Cogs & Chainrings												
Chain: Check for Wear												
Derailleur: Lube Pivots & Pulleys												
Drivetrain: Degrease & Lube												
Pedals: Lube & Tighten												
Saddle												
Shift Cables: Lube												
Structural Inspection												
Suspension Bolts & Forks												
Suspension Sliders: Lube												
Tighten Nuts, Bolts &Fasteners												
Wheels & Tires: Condition, Pressure & Spokes												
Wipe Down & Clean Bike												

ANNUAL MAINTENANCE CHECK

SERVICE ITEM	✓
Accessories: Check, Update or Replacement	
Bleed Hydraulic Brakes	
Bottom Bracket Overhaul or Replacement	
Brake Pad Replacement	
Cable & Housing Replacement	
Chain: Deep clean or Replacement	
Derailleur: Clean Jockey Wheels	
Frame & Dropper Post Overhaul	
Frame: Clean & Wax	
Handlebar Tape or Grips Replacement	
Headset Overhaul	
Hubs Overhaul	
Pedal Overhaul	
Shock Oil Replacement	
Suspension Pivots: Clean & Grease	
Tire Replacement	
Tubeless Tire Sealant Replacement	
Wheels: True Alignment & Tension	

MONTHLY MAINTENANCE CHECK

YEAR:	JANUARY	FEBRUARY	MARCH	APRIL	MAY	JUNE	JULY	AUGUST	SEPTEMBER	OCTOBER	NOVEMBER	DECEMBER
Brake Cables: Lube												
Brake Pads, Cable Clamp & Levers												
Chain, Cogs & Chainrings												
Chain: Check for Wear												
Derailleur: Lube Pivots & Pulleys												
Drivetrain: Degrease & Lube												
Pedals: Lube & Tighten												
Saddle												
Shift Cables: Lube												
Structural Inspection												
Suspension Bolts & Forks												
Suspension Sliders: Lube												
Tighten Nuts, Bolts &Fasteners												
Wheels & Tires: Condition, Pressure & Spokes												
Wipe Down & Clean Bike												

🚲 ANNUAL MAINTENANCE CHECK 🚲

SERVICE ITEM	✓
Accessories: Check, Update or Replacement	
Bleed Hydraulic Brakes	
Bottom Bracket Overhaul or Replacement	
Brake Pad Replacement	
Cable & Housing Replacement	
Chain: Deep clean or Replacement	
Derailleur: Clean Jockey Wheels	
Frame & Dropper Post Overhaul	
Frame: Clean & Wax	
Handlebar Tape or Grips Replacement	
Headset Overhaul	
Hubs Overhaul	
Pedal Overhaul	
Shock Oil Replacement	
Suspension Pivots: Clean & Grease	
Tire Replacement	
Tubeless Tire Sealant Replacement	
Wheels: True Alignment & Tension	

MONTHLY MAINTENANCE CHECK

YEAR:	JANUARY	FEBRUARY	MARCH	APRIL	MAY	JUNE	JULY	AUGUST	SEPTEMBER	OCTOBER	NOVEMBER	DECEMBER
Brake Cables: Lube												
Brake Pads, Cable Clamp & Levers												
Chain, Cogs & Chainrings												
Chain: Check for Wear												
Derailleur: Lube Pivots & Pulleys												
Drivetrain: Degrease & Lube												
Pedals: Lube & Tighten												
Saddle												
Shift Cables: Lube												
Structural Inspection												
Suspension Bolts & Forks												
Suspension Sliders: Lube												
Tighten Nuts, Bolts &Fasteners												
Wheels & Tires: Condition, Pressure & Spokes												
Wipe Down & Clean Bike												

🚴 ANNUAL MAINTENANCE CHECK 🚴

SERVICE ITEM	✓
Accessories: Check, Update or Replacement	
Bleed Hydraulic Brakes	
Bottom Bracket Overhaul or Replacement	
Brake Pad Replacement	
Cable & Housing Replacement	
Chain: Deep clean or Replacement	
Derailleur: Clean Jockey Wheels	
Frame & Dropper Post Overhaul	
Frame: Clean & Wax	
Handlebar Tape or Grips Replacement	
Headset Overhaul	
Hubs Overhaul	
Pedal Overhaul	
Shock Oil Replacement	
Suspension Pivots: Clean & Grease	
Tire Replacement	
Tubeless Tire Sealant Replacement	
Wheels: True Alignment & Tension	

MONTHLY MAINTENANCE CHECK

YEAR: ✓	JANUARY	FEBRUARY	MARCH	APRIL	MAY	JUNE	JULY	AUGUST	SEPTEMBER	OCTOBER	NOVEMBER	DECEMBER
Brake Cables: Lube												
Brake Pads, Cable Clamp & Levers												
Chain, Cogs & Chainrings												
Chain: Check for Wear												
Derailleur: Lube Pivots & Pulleys												
Drivetrain: Degrease & Lube												
Pedals: Lube & Tighten												
Saddle												
Shift Cables: Lube												
Structural Inspection												
Suspension Bolts & Forks												
Suspension Sliders: Lube												
Tighten Nuts, Bolts &Fasteners												
Wheels & Tires: Condition, Pressure & Spokes												
Wipe Down & Clean Bike												

🚲 ANNUAL MAINTENANCE CHECK 🚲

SERVICE ITEM	✓
Accessories: Check, Update or Replacement	
Bleed Hydraulic Brakes	
Bottom Bracket Overhaul or Replacement	
Brake Pad Replacement	
Cable & Housing Replacement	
Chain: Deep clean or Replacement	
Derailleur: Clean Jockey Wheels	
Frame & Dropper Post Overhaul	
Frame: Clean & Wax	
Handlebar Tape or Grips Replacement	
Headset Overhaul	
Hubs Overhaul	
Pedal Overhaul	
Shock Oil Replacement	
Suspension Pivots: Clean & Grease	
Tire Replacement	
Tubeless Tire Sealant Replacement	
Wheels: True Alignment & Tension	

MONTHLY MAINTENANCE CHECK

YEAR:	JANUARY	FEBRUARY	MARCH	APRIL	MAY	JUNE	JULY	AUGUST	SEPTEMBER	OCTOBER	NOVEMBER	DECEMBER
Brake Cables: Lube												
Brake Pads, Cable Clamp & Levers												
Chain, Cogs & Chainrings												
Chain: Check for Wear												
Derailleur: Lube Pivots & Pulleys												
Drivetrain: Degrease & Lube												
Pedals: Lube & Tighten												
Saddle												
Shift Cables: Lube												
Structural Inspection												
Suspension Bolts & Forks												
Suspension Sliders: Lube												
Tighten Nuts, Bolts &Fasteners												
Wheels & Tires: Condition, Pressure & Spokes												
Wipe Down & Clean Bike												

ANNUAL MAINTENANCE CHECK

SERVICE ITEM	✓
Accessories: Check, Update or Replacement	
Bleed Hydraulic Brakes	
Bottom Bracket Overhaul or Replacement	
Brake Pad Replacement	
Cable & Housing Replacement	
Chain: Deep clean or Replacement	
Derailleur: Clean Jockey Wheels	
Frame & Dropper Post Overhaul	
Frame: Clean & Wax	
Handlebar Tape or Grips Replacement	
Headset Overhaul	
Hubs Overhaul	
Pedal Overhaul	
Shock Oil Replacement	
Suspension Pivots: Clean & Grease	
Tire Replacement	
Tubeless Tire Sealant Replacement	
Wheels: True Alignment & Tension	

MONTHLY MAINTENANCE CHECK

YEAR:	JANUARY	FEBRUARY	MARCH	APRIL	MAY	JUNE	JULY	AUGUST	SEPTEMBER	OCTOBER	NOVEMBER	DECEMBER
Brake Cables: Lube												
Brake Pads, Cable Clamp & Levers												
Chain, Cogs & Chainrings												
Chain: Check for Wear												
Derailleur: Lube Pivots & Pulleys												
Drivetrain: Degrease & Lube												
Pedals: Lube & Tighten												
Saddle												
Shift Cables: Lube												
Structural Inspection												
Suspension Bolts & Forks												
Suspension Sliders: Lube												
Tighten Nuts, Bolts &Fasteners												
Wheels & Tires: Condition, Pressure & Spokes												
Wipe Down & Clean Bike												

🚲 ANNUAL MAINTENANCE CHECK 🚲

SERVICE ITEM	✓
Accessories: Check, Update or Replacement	
Bleed Hydraulic Brakes	
Bottom Bracket Overhaul or Replacement	
Brake Pad Replacement	
Cable & Housing Replacement	
Chain: Deep clean or Replacement	
Derailleur: Clean Jockey Wheels	
Frame & Dropper Post Overhaul	
Frame: Clean & Wax	
Handlebar Tape or Grips Replacement	
Headset Overhaul	
Hubs Overhaul	
Pedal Overhaul	
Shock Oil Replacement	
Suspension Pivots: Clean & Grease	
Tire Replacement	
Tubeless Tire Sealant Replacement	
Wheels: True Alignment & Tension	

MONTHLY MAINTENANCE CHECK

YEAR:	JANUARY	FEBRUARY	MARCH	APRIL	MAY	JUNE	JULY	AUGUST	SEPTEMBER	OCTOBER	NOVEMBER	DECEMBER
Brake Cables: Lube												
Brake Pads, Cable Clamp & Levers												
Chain, Cogs & Chainrings												
Chain: Check for Wear												
Derailleur: Lube Pivots & Pulleys												
Drivetrain: Degrease & Lube												
Pedals: Lube & Tighten												
Saddle												
Shift Cables: Lube												
Structural Inspection												
Suspension Bolts & Forks												
Suspension Sliders: Lube												
Tighten Nuts, Bolts &Fasteners												
Wheels & Tires: Condition, Pressure & Spokes												
Wipe Down & Clean Bike												

ANNUAL MAINTENANCE CHECK

SERVICE ITEM	✓
Accessories: Check, Update or Replacement	
Bleed Hydraulic Brakes	
Bottom Bracket Overhaul or Replacement	
Brake Pad Replacement	
Cable & Housing Replacement	
Chain: Deep clean or Replacement	
Derailleur: Clean Jockey Wheels	
Frame & Dropper Post Overhaul	
Frame: Clean & Wax	
Handlebar Tape or Grips Replacement	
Headset Overhaul	
Hubs Overhaul	
Pedal Overhaul	
Shock Oil Replacement	
Suspension Pivots: Clean & Grease	
Tire Replacement	
Tubeless Tire Sealant Replacement	
Wheels: True Alignment & Tension	

MONTHLY MAINTENANCE CHECK

YEAR: ✓	JANUARY	FEBRUARY	MARCH	APRIL	MAY	JUNE	JULY	AUGUST	SEPTEMBER	OCTOBER	NOVEMBER	DECEMBER
Brake Cables: Lube												
Brake Pads, Cable Clamp & Levers												
Chain, Cogs & Chainrings												
Chain: Check for Wear												
Derailleur: Lube Pivots & Pulleys												
Drivetrain: Degrease & Lube												
Pedals: Lube & Tighten												
Saddle												
Shift Cables: Lube												
Structural Inspection												
Suspension Bolts & Forks												
Suspension Sliders: Lube												
Tighten Nuts, Bolts &Fasteners												
Wheels & Tires: Condition, Pressure & Spokes												
Wipe Down & Clean Bike												

ANNUAL MAINTENANCE CHECK

SERVICE ITEM	✓
Accessories: Check, Update or Replacement	
Bleed Hydraulic Brakes	
Bottom Bracket Overhaul or Replacement	
Brake Pad Replacement	
Cable & Housing Replacement	
Chain: Deep clean or Replacement	
Derailleur: Clean Jockey Wheels	
Frame & Dropper Post Overhaul	
Frame: Clean & Wax	
Handlebar Tape or Grips Replacement	
Headset Overhaul	
Hubs Overhaul	
Pedal Overhaul	
Shock Oil Replacement	
Suspension Pivots: Clean & Grease	
Tire Replacement	
Tubeless Tire Sealant Replacement	
Wheels: True Alignment & Tension	

MONTHLY MAINTENANCE CHECK

YEAR: ✓	JANUARY	FEBRUARY	MARCH	APRIL	MAY	JUNE	JULY	AUGUST	SEPTEMBER	OCTOBER	NOVEMBER	DECEMBER
Brake Cables: Lube												
Brake Pads, Cable Clamp & Levers												
Chain, Cogs & Chainrings												
Chain: Check for Wear												
Derailleur: Lube Pivots & Pulleys												
Drivetrain: Degrease & Lube												
Pedals: Lube & Tighten												
Saddle												
Shift Cables: Lube												
Structural Inspection												
Suspension Bolts & Forks												
Suspension Sliders: Lube												
Tighten Nuts, Bolts &Fasteners												
Wheels & Tires: Condition, Pressure & Spokes												
Wipe Down & Clean Bike												

ANNUAL MAINTENANCE CHECK

SERVICE ITEM	✓
Accessories: Check, Update or Replacement	
Bleed Hydraulic Brakes	
Bottom Bracket Overhaul or Replacement	
Brake Pad Replacement	
Cable & Housing Replacement	
Chain: Deep clean or Replacement	
Derailleur: Clean Jockey Wheels	
Frame & Dropper Post Overhaul	
Frame: Clean & Wax	
Handlebar Tape or Grips Replacement	
Headset Overhaul	
Hubs Overhaul	
Pedal Overhaul	
Shock Oil Replacement	
Suspension Pivots: Clean & Grease	
Tire Replacement	
Tubeless Tire Sealant Replacement	
Wheels: True Alignment & Tension	

BICYCLE REPAIRS LOG

DATE	MILEAGE	SERVICED BY	DETAILS	COST

BICYCLE REPAIRS LOG

DATE	MILEAGE	SERVICED BY	DETAILS	COST

BICYCLE REPAIRS LOG

DATE	MILEAGE	SERVICED BY	DETAILS	COST

BICYCLE REPAIRS LOG

DATE	MILEAGE	SERVICED BY	DETAILS	COST

BICYCLE REPAIRS LOG

DATE	MILEAGE	SERVICED BY	DETAILS	COST

BICYCLE REPAIRS LOG

DATE	MILEAGE	SERVICED BY	DETAILS	COST

BICYCLE REPAIRS LOG

DATE	MILEAGE	SERVICED BY	DETAILS	COST

BICYCLE REPAIRS LOG

DATE	MILEAGE	SERVICED BY	DETAILS	COST

BICYCLE REPAIRS LOG

DATE	MILEAGE	SERVICED BY	DETAILS	COST

BICYCLE REPAIRS LOG

DATE	MILEAGE	SERVICED BY	DETAILS	COST

🚲 RIDE CYCLOCOMPUTER LOG 🚲

DATE	DISTANCE	DURATION	AVE/MAX SPEED	ELEVATION	HEART RATE	DESTINATION OR RIDE NAME

RIDE CYCLOCOMPUTER LOG

DATE	DISTANCE	DURATION	AVE/MAX SPEED	ELEVATION	HEART RATE	DESTINATION OR RIDE NAME

RIDE CYCLOCOMPUTER LOG

DATE	DISTANCE	DURATION	AVE/MAX SPEED	ELEVATION	HEART RATE	DESTINATION OR RIDE NAME

RIDE CYCLOCOMPUTER LOG

DATE	DISTANCE	DURATION	AVE/MAX SPEED	ELEVATION	HEART RATE	DESTINATION OR RIDE NAME

RIDE CYCLOCOMPUTER LOG

DATE	DISTANCE	DURATION	AVE/MAX SPEED	ELEVATION	HEART RATE	DESTINATION OR RIDE NAME

RIDE CYCLOCOMPUTER LOG

DATE	DISTANCE	DURATION	AVE/MAX SPEED	ELEVATION	HEART RATE	DESTINATION OR RIDE NAME

RIDE CYCLOCOMPUTER LOG

DATE	DISTANCE	DURATION	AVE/MAX SPEED	ELEVATION	HEART RATE	DESTINATION OR RIDE NAME

RIDE CYCLOCOMPUTER LOG

DATE	DISTANCE	DURATION	AVE/MAX SPEED	ELEVATION	HEART RATE	DESTINATION OR RIDE NAME

RIDE CYCLOCOMPUTER LOG

DATE	DISTANCE	DURATION	AVE/MAX SPEED	ELEVATION	HEART RATE	DESTINATION OR RIDE NAME

RIDE CYCLOCOMPUTER LOG

DATE	DISTANCE	DURATION	AVE/MAX SPEED	ELEVATION	HEART RATE	DESTINATION OR RIDE NAME

🚴 RIDE CYCLOCOMPUTER LOG 🚴

DATE	DISTANCE	DURATION	AVE/MAX SPEED	ELEVATION	HEART RATE	DESTINATION OR RIDE NAME

RIDE CYCLOCOMPUTER LOG

DATE	DISTANCE	DURATION	AVE/MAX SPEED	ELEVATION	HEART RATE	DESTINATION OR RIDE NAME

🚴 RIDE CYCLOCOMPUTER LOG 🚴

DATE	DISTANCE	DURATION	AVE/MAX SPEED	ELEVATION	HEART RATE	DESTINATION OR RIDE NAME

RIDE CYCLOCOMPUTER LOG

DATE	DISTANCE	DURATION	AVE/MAX SPEED	ELEVATION	HEART RATE	DESTINATION OR RIDE NAME

🚴 RIDE CYCLOCOMPUTER LOG 🚴

DATE	DISTANCE	DURATION	AVE/MAX SPEED	ELEVATION	HEART RATE	DESTINATION OR RIDE NAME

🚴 RIDE CYCLOCOMPUTER LOG 🚴

DATE	DISTANCE	DURATION	AVE/MAX SPEED	ELEVATION	HEART RATE	DESTINATION OR RIDE NAME

🚴 RIDE CYCLOCOMPUTER LOG 🚴

DATE	DISTANCE	DURATION	AVE/MAX SPEED	ELEVATION	HEART RATE	DESTINATION OR RIDE NAME

RIDE CYCLOCOMPUTER LOG

DATE	DISTANCE	DURATION	AVE/MAX SPEED	ELEVATION	HEART RATE	DESTINATION OR RIDE NAME

RIDE CYCLOCOMPUTER LOG

DATE	DISTANCE	DURATION	AVE/MAX SPEED	ELEVATION	HEART RATE	DESTINATION OR RIDE NAME

RIDE CYCLOCOMPUTER LOG

DATE	DISTANCE	DURATION	AVE/MAX SPEED	ELEVATION	HEART RATE	DESTINATION OR RIDE NAME

RIDE CYCLOCOMPUTER LOG

DATE	DISTANCE	DURATION	AVE/MAX SPEED	ELEVATION	HEART RATE	DESTINATION OR RIDE NAME

RIDE CYCLOCOMPUTER LOG

DATE	DISTANCE	DURATION	AVE/MAX SPEED	ELEVATION	HEART RATE	DESTINATION OR RIDE NAME

🚲 RIDE CYCLOCOMPUTER LOG 🚲

DATE	DISTANCE	DURATION	AVE/MAX SPEED	ELEVATION	HEART RATE	DESTINATION OR RIDE NAME

RIDE CYCLOCOMPUTER LOG

DATE	DISTANCE	DURATION	AVE/MAX SPEED	ELEVATION	HEART RATE	DESTINATION OR RIDE NAME

🚴 RIDE CYCLOCOMPUTER LOG 🚴

DATE	DISTANCE	DURATION	AVE/MAX SPEED	ELEVATION	HEART RATE	DESTINATION OR RIDE NAME

RIDE CYCLOCOMPUTER LOG

DATE	DISTANCE	DURATION	AVE/MAX SPEED	ELEVATION	HEART RATE	DESTINATION OR RIDE NAME

RIDE CYCLOCOMPUTER LOG

DATE	DISTANCE	DURATION	AVE/MAX SPEED	ELEVATION	HEART RATE	DESTINATION OR RIDE NAME

RIDE CYCLOCOMPUTER LOG

DATE	DISTANCE	DURATION	AVE/MAX SPEED	ELEVATION	HEART RATE	DESTINATION OR RIDE NAME

🚲 RIDE CYCLOCOMPUTER LOG 🚲

DATE	DISTANCE	DURATION	AVE/MAX SPEED	ELEVATION	HEART RATE	DESTINATION OR RIDE NAME

Printed in Great Britain
by Amazon